Ten-Minute Real World Reading

by Murray Suid

illustrated by Philip Chalk

Publisher: Roberta Suid
Editor: Hawkeye McMorrow
Design & Production: Scott McMorrow

Other Monday Morning publications by the author: *Book Factory, For the Love of Research, How to Be an Inventor, How to Be President of the U.S.A., Picture Book Factory, Report Factory, Storybooks Teach Writing, Ten-Minute Grammar Grabbers, Ten-Minute Editing Skill Builders, Ten-Minute Thinking Tie-ins, Ten-Minute Real World Writing*

For a complete catalog, please write to the address above,
or visit our Web site: www.mondaymorningbooks.com
e-mail: MMBooks@aol.com

ISBN 1-57612-022-8

Printed in the United States of America
987654321

CONTENTS

INTRODUCTION

Aesop's fable of "The Hare and the Tortoise" teaches us that slow and steady leads to success. This is surely true with literacy. Mastery requires thoughtful practice spread over a long time.

Ten-Minute Real World Reading follows this patient approach. The book offers dozens of short, skill-building activities designed to fit into the busy school day.

Skills and Applications

The lessons in this book cover key comprehension and fluency skills for both nonfiction and fiction. These include:
• grasping the big idea
• spotting details
• uncovering implicit meanings
• focusing on relevant data
• using context clues
• predicting outcomes
• asking critical questions
• making comparisons

Such skills gain meaning when used in authentic contexts. Thus, in Part 1, **Everyday Reading**, you'll find activities related to dozens of formats encountered in daily life, such as advertisements, menus, rules, emergency information cards, and tables. A number of these projects, such as Responsive Reading and Readers' Theater, emphasize oral language techniques. Online Interviews and TV News Copy provide experience in multimedia.

Although most of the activities here and throughout the book can be done solo, several lessons involve small or large groups. A prime example is Choral Reading.

Part 2, **Fiction**, develops awareness of nine important elements of fiction, including characterization, point of view, and theme. These concepts are equally relevant whether students are reading short stories or novels. The information gained in this section can also help young writers create more interesting stories themselves.

Part 3, **Study Skills**, links reading to a variety of academic tasks, such as comparing, paraphrasing, and reading recall.

How to Use the Book

Each lesson consists of a few simple teaching steps. Most lessons include a **reproducible reading sample**. For example, the lesson on responsive reading includes three passages that students can perform in small groups. The readings are drawn from all subject areas, in order to emphasize that language arts skills serve the entire curriculum.

The **Resources** section at the back of the book begins with a reproducible Reader's Guide packed with information of value to lifelong reading. Written for students, it covers such topics as:
• avoiding eyestrain
• taking care of books
• intelligently approaching newspaper articles
• skimming
• proofreading
• keeping a reading journal

One of the most important items in the Reader's Guide is a simple checklist for determining if one has truly grasped a book.

Resources also includes a dozen reading experiences that can continue throughout the entire year, adding continuity to your literacy program. Examples are:
• sponsoring book groups
• getting the most out of author correspondence
• reading as a means of world exploration

You'll also find a list of book report projects, ranging from classic newspaper-style reviews to dioramas.

Beyond Ten Minutes

Each lesson includes an extension project that reinforces the main concept. These in-depth activities can be used for independent study at school or at home. Frequently, there's a direct link to writing.

Online Sharing

You can find additional free reading resources on our Web site: **www.mondaymorningbooks.com**. There, we'll post interesting links to sites around the world, and also additional activities as we develop them. If you're not on the Net, ask a colleague (or student) to download items for you.

If you have questions or comments you'd like to share electronically with other teachers, write **mmbooks@aol.com**.

ADVERTISEMENTS

Learning to make sense out of advertisements provides practice in critical thinking.

DIRECTIONS:
1. Give each student a copy of the sample advertisement, next page.
2. Have students read the advertisement and answer the questions on a separate sheet of paper.
3. Discuss the answers. Point out some of the slippery language and unsubstantiated claims. For example, while Bestway bicycles might be made of the finest materials, other bicycles might be made of the same materials.

EXTENSION:
Have students collect ads from newspapers and magazines, and then write advertisement reports that analyze the messages. These reports can be shared orally or on a bulletin board. Students might also send their comments to the advertisers.

Answers for next page:
1. No 2. Ten colors 3. Yes 4. Can't tell 5. Can't tell
6. Can't tell 7. Can't tell 8. The advertiser

Sample Advertisement

Read the following advertisement. Then answer the questions below.

> ## Buy a Bestway Bicycle for the Ride of Your Life
>
> Some people are satisfied with any old bicycle. But our Bestway bicycles are made for people who really love to ride. Serious bicyclists know that our bicycles are best because:
> - They're made of the finest materials.
> - They're tested under all conditions.
> - They last longer than most other bikes.
> - They come in 10 vibrant colors.
> - They have great balance.
> - They offer pillow-soft seats.
> - They feature "Sure-Stop" brakes.
>
> If you love bicycling, you'll love riding a Bestway Bike, the best bicycle in the world.

Questions:
1. Can you tell how well Bestway bicycles have done when tested?
2. How many colors do Bestway bicycles come in?
3. Is it possible that some brands last longer than Bestway bikes?
4. Do Bestway bicycles come in more colors than other brands?
5. Do Bestway bicycles have better balance than other bicycles?
6. Are Bestway seats more comfortable than seats on other bicycles?
7. What's good about "Sure-Stop Brakes"?
8. Who says Bestway Bikes are the "best" in the world?

Ten-Minute Real World Reading ©1997 Monday Morning Books, Inc.

CHORAL READING

Reading aloud in a group can help shy students overcome stage fright and lay the foundation for effective public speaking.

DIRECTIONS:
1. Explain that choral reading involves two or more performers reading aloud a passage at the same time. Listening to a "lead reader" enables the group to stay together.
2. Divide the class into three groups. Choose a leader for each group.
3. Give each group copies of a reading, such as those on the Choral Reading Cards, next page.
4. Provide a few minutes for the groups to rehearse their readings two or three times. They should keep their voices low to avoid disturbing the other groups.
5. Have each group move to the front of the room to present.

EXTENSION:
Repeat the activity using materials chosen by the students. Encourage students to experiment with passages from a variety of fiction and nonfiction genres, as well as poetry. Also, try different-sized groups.

Choral Reading Cards

Poem

How doth the little crocodile
Improve his shining tail,
And pour the waters of the Nile
On every golden scale!
How cheerfully he seems to grin,
How neatly spreads his claws,
And welcomes little fishes in
With gently smiling jaws!
    Lewis Carroll

Fable

One day a fox fell into a well. He struggled to keep his head above water. Then he heard footsteps. He looked up and saw a wolf at the top of the well.

The wolf said, "Oh, poor fox, I feel so sorry to see you in this trouble." Tears begin to roll down the wolf's snout.

The fox said, "Wolf, it is kind of you to be sorry for me. But if you really want to help, don't just stand there. Go find a rope and pull me up."

The moral is: Action speaks louder than words.

    Aesop

A Fact About Your Heart

Where is your heart? Try this. Put your hand over the place where you think the heart is.

If you're like most people, your hand is on the left side of your body. You might feel something going thump thump, thump thump. But it is not your heart. It's a big blood vessel called the aorta. The aorta carries blood from the heart throughout the body. But the heart itself lies mainly in the middle of your chest. If your hand isn't in the middle, move it there now.

Adapted from an encyclopedia

Ten-Minute Real World Reading ©1997 Monday Morning Books, Inc.

CLASSIFIED ADS

Classified ads are like condensed soup. You have to "expand" them before using.

DIRECTIONS:
1. Give each student a copy of the sample classified ads, next page.
2. Explain that newspapers charge advertisers for the space they use. That's why classified ad writers shrink their messages by translating them into a kind of code that omits words and letters.
3. Optional: On the board show how to translate a classified ad into plain English. For example, write:

> Lost: Pocket watch. Silver case. Fam keepsake.
> Bg reward.

Then add the omitted words and spell out the abbreviations:

> I lost a pocket watch, which has a silver case. It's a
> family keepsake. If you return it, I'll give you a big reward.

Explain that there are other ways to rewrite the same ad.
4. Have students translate one or more of the ads using complete sentences and spelling out abbreviations.
5. Students can share their work in small groups or on the board.

EXTENSION:
Have students write classified ads that might have been placed by characters in well-known stories.

I'd like to place a classified ad about a glass slipper I found.

Classified Advertisements to Rewrite

Rewrite the following advertisements as complete sentences. Fill in the missing words, and spell out every abbreviation.

1. Lost: Pocket watch. Silver case. Fam keepsake. Bg reward.

2. Found: Gld rng. in Food Mart pkng lot, Sept. 18.

3. For sale: 10-spd bike. Gd cond. Blue frame, gold trim. Front/rear lights. Kept inside. Must sell.

4. For sale: Six old radios. One works. All made before 1940. Best offer.

5. Free: Tent. Sleeps 4. All parts incl. Needs 2 or 3 patches.

6. Job Wanted as short order cook. Can make pncakes, waffles, eggs, biscuits, rolls, sndwiches. Soups my specialty. Fst. Clean. Hrd wrking. Never sick. E-z to get along with. A.M., P.M., wkends OK.

7. Actors Wanted 4 play about talking animals. Need unusual voices. Tryouts Tues. eve. Rehearsals last 1 mnth. 4 performances. No pay.

"Fnd. 1 gl. slpr @ ball Sat nt. Pls call castle eves. if yrs."

It says that someone found one glass slipper at the ball held on Saturday night. The finder says, "Please call the castle in the evening if the slipper is yours."

DIAGRAMS

Knowing how to read diagrams is an important study skill. It's also useful in everyday situations, such as assembling toys and using household products.

DIRECTIONS:
1. Give each student or small group a copy of the Sample Diagram, next page. You might also use diagrams from textbooks and other publications.
2. Point out the four elements found in many diagrams:
• title
• art
• caption: a short overview of the subject
• labels: words that name the subject's parts
3. Give students a few minutes to answer the questions about the diagram.
4. Discuss their responses.

EXTENSION:
Have students diagram objects that they use in their lives. Examples include musical instruments, eating utensils, school tools, clothing, and sports equipment. These diagrams can later be used to illustrate written or oral reports.

— Maybe we should have studied the diagram.

EASY TO ASSEMBLE

Answers for next page:
1. The spiral thread 2. The hub 3. To catch insects
4. Yes 5. The bridge 6. There are many possible answers, for example: "How a Spider Spins Her Web."

Sample Diagram

Study the diagram. Then answer the questions below.

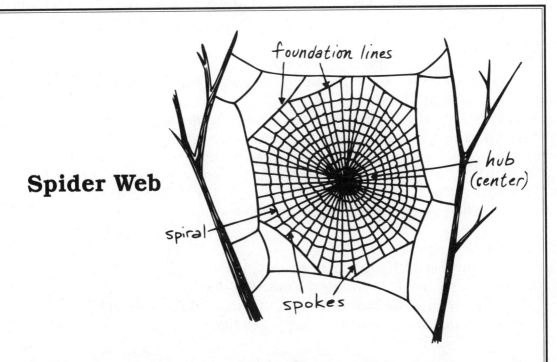

Spider Web
(labeled: foundation lines, hub (center), spiral, spokes)

Only female spiders spin webs. Different kinds of spiders work differently, but here's a common method.

The spider first lays a thread between two supports, for example, stems of a plant. This bridge is one of several long strands, known as foundation lines.

Next, the spider spins spoke-like threads from one side of the web to the other.

Finally, starting at the center, the spider spins a sticky spiral thread. Insects that fly into the web get stuck on this sticky strand. The spider avoids getting caught by walking on the non-sticky threads.

Questions:
1. What part of the web is sticky?
2. What is the other name for the center of the web?
3. What is the job of the spiral?
4. Does every spoke connect to a foundation line?
5. Which part of a web is spun out first?
6. What would be a more specific or interesting title for this diagram? (Use seven or fewer words in the new title.)

EMERGENCY INFORMATION

Most reading materials provide education or entertainment. But some reading materials deal with matters of life and death.

DIRECTIONS:
1. Explain that hotels, airlines, and other businesses often provide safety information. It's the customer's responsibility to read and think about this material.
2. Divide the class into small groups. Give each group a copy of the Sample Emergency Information handout, next page.
3. Have students study the information and answer the questions.
4. Go over the answers with the class. You might use this time to show students warning messages printed on things like bleach containers and fire extinguishers.

EXTENSION:
Have students research and write emergency preparation cards for their homes. Topics might include fires, floods, earthquakes, and storms. When finished, the cards can be taken home for family reading.

> **Answers for next page:**
> 1. Room 403 2. West Exit 3. To avoid getting cuts 4. The power might stop in a fire, trapping people inside the elevator.

Sample Emergency Information

Study the hotel fire emergency card, and then answer the questions below.

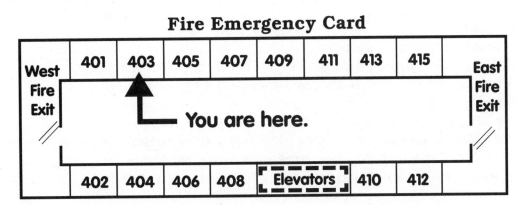

Fire Emergency Card

Please study the picture and information on this card.

1. Locate the two nearest emergency exits. In case of a fire, DO NOT use an elevator.

2. If you hear a ringing bell, prepare to leave your room immediately. Be sure to have shoes on in case you encounter broken glass or other debris.

3. Take your room key.

4. Go to the door and feel it.

 • Open the door slowly. If the way is clear, walk quickly to the closest fire exit. Open the fire exit door. If the way is clear, walk down the stairs and leave the building. If the stairwell is filled with smoke, return to the hallway and walk to the next closest emergency exit. If this stairwell is clear, walk down and exit the building. Otherwise, return to your room.

 • If when you open the door, smoke or flames block your way to all exits, close your door quickly. Place a wet towel at the bottom of the door to keep smoke from entering the room. Dampen other towels to use as filters for breathing.

Questions:

1. What room is this card for?
2. Which fire exit is closest to the room?
3. Why do you think it's important to put on shoes before leaving the room?
4. Why do you think there's a warning against using the elevators during a fire emergency?

GAME RULES

Knowing how to figure out games is a lifelong skill that sharpens attention to detail. It also offers practice in following other kinds of directions.

DIRECTIONS:
1. Divide the class into pairs.
2. Give each pair of the Number Toe rules, next page. Number Toe is a math game, which involves more strategy than traditional tic-tac-toe.
3. Have students read the rules and play a test game.
4. Later, ask for two volunteers to play a demonstration game on the board. This way you can make sure that everyone understands the rules. Invite students to teach the game to their family members and friends.

EXTENSION:
Have students write out rules for games they are familiar with, and then share the rules on a bulletin board.

Sample Game Rules

Read the following rules. Then, to check your understanding of the rules, play a game with a partner.

Number Toe Rules

1. This math game is for two players.
2. The game is played on a grid that looks like a tic-tac-toe pattern (Diagram A).
3. The goal is to complete any row, column, or diagonal so that any two of the numbers in that line add up to the third. The order of the numbers does not matter. The first player to complete a line wins.
4. Begin play by drawing a grid.
5. Have one player put a number (from 0 to 12) in any box. Once a number is played, it CANNOT be used again in the game.
6. Have the second player put a different number in another box (Diagram B).
7. If possible, the first player wins the game by completing a row, column, or diagonal. Or the player puts a number in an unused box (Diagram C).
8. Continue until one player wins the game (Diagram D) or until no further moves are possible, in which the game is tied.

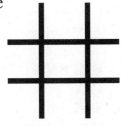

Diagram A

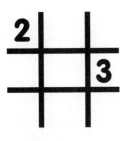

Diagram B

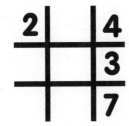

Diagram C

Diagram D

 Ten-Minute Real World Reading ©1997 Monday Morning Books, Inc.

GUARANTEES

Sellers often use the word "guarantee" to entice people to buy their products. But smart shoppers know that it's important to read the "small print" to see if the guarantee is really worth anything.

DIRECTIONS:
1. Discuss the meaning of the word "guarantee." It means a promise that a product or service will satisfy the customer. Explain that guarantees often come with conditions that can make it difficult for unhappy buyers to get satisfaction.
2. Give each student a copy of the Sample Guarantee, next page. Point out that the conditions are printed in small, hard-to-read type.
3. Have students read the guarantee and answer the questions.
4. Discuss the answers in class.

EXTENSION:
Have students collect and make a bulletin board of guarantees that appear on packages for household products.

Answers for next page:
1. The company 2. No 3. No 4. The customer 5. No 6. The small print hides some of the conditions. The customer might not realize that the guarantee favors the company. 7. Open ended question

Sample Guarantee

Read the guarantee. Then answer the questions below.

Lifetime Guarantee

Congratulations. You are the lucky owner of a new Timeless Watch. A **Timeless Watch** is made so well that it will last practically forever.

That's why we can offer you this amazing guarantee: IF THE WATCH EVER STOPS KEEPING ACCURATE TIME because of a defect, simply mail it to us at the address on the box, and we'll repair it for free or send you a new one at no cost to you.

Conditions:

1. This guarantee does not cover damage caused by falls, fire, water, or improper use.

2. The guarantee covers only the original owner.

3. The guarantee is good only if the owner used the watch according to all directions in the manual that came with the watch.

4. "Keeping accurate time" means that the watch gains or loses no more than two minutes a week.

5. The owner will pay the cost of shipping the product to the Timeless Watch factory.

6. The original purchase receipt must accompany the watch being returned.

7. The Timeless Watch company reserves the right to decide if a watch has been improperly used and therefore not covered by this guarantee.

8. After sending a watch to the company, allow six weeks for a response.

Questions:

1. Who decides if the watch has been properly used?
2. If the watch loses one hour a year, will it be repaired for free?
3. If you can't find the receipt that came when the watch was bought, can you still ask the company to repair it for free?
4. Who pays for returning a broken watch to the company?
5. If you decide that you don't want the watch any more and give it to a friend, is the guarantee still good?
6. Why do you think the conditions are printed in small type?
7. Do you think the conditions are fair? Explain why or why not.

INDEXES

Being able to understand and use indexes is a key to library research. More and more, it's also an essential skill for using computers and the Internet.

DIRECTIONS:
1. Give each student a copy of the Sample Index, next page.
2. Optional: If students are not familiar with indexes, give them a quick overview:
• An index is an alphabetical list of topics in a book.
• It makes it easy for readers to find specific information.
• Each word or phrase in an index is called an "entry." Often, there will be more than one entry related to a single topic. For example, in the sample index, several entries deal with bees, such as "hives" and "queen bees."
3. Have students answer the questions about the index.
4. Discuss the answers.

EXTENSION:
For a book report, have students choose books with indexes, and then discuss how well the indexes work.

Answers for next page:
1. One page 2. Three pages: p. 3 (flight), p. 4 (locomotion), p. 5 (speed) 3. Diseases, poisonous insects 4. Open ended
5. There are many, for example, crickets, gnats, and wasps.

Sample Index

Read the following index, and then answer the questions.

antennae, 46
ants, 23-25
beehives, 29
bees, 27-30
beetles, 5, 9, 27
body parts, 4
butterflies, 43-46
bugs, 2
camouflage, 3, 15, 19
classification, 60-64
cocoons, 45
diseases,
    caused by insects, 17, 25
    of insects, 38
entomology, 2
exoskeleton, 4, 63
fireflies, 47
fleas, 39
flies, 21-23
flight, 3
food, 4, 14, 27, 28
grasshoppers, 18
habitats, 2-4
history, 1, 2
hives, 29
honeybees, 27, 28
horseflies, 23

houseflies, 21, 22
insecticide, 4
insects as food, 8, 18
ladybugs, 2, 5, 9
larva, 7
legs, 4
life cycle of insects, 7-9
locomotion, 4
longevity, 9
mosquitoes, 4, 23, 24
moths, 43-46
myths about insects, 1
pets, 2
poems about insects, 65-68
poisonous insects, 5
pollination, 28
praying mantis, 42
pupa, 8
queen bees, 27
relatives, 60-64
size, 3
skeleton, 2
speed, 5
termites, 37
ticks, 2
uses of, 1-3, 18, 19, 27
vision, 4

Questions
1. How many pages in the book deal with the size of insects?
2. How many entries deal with the way insects move? List them.
3. Which entries deal with problems that insects cause humans?
4. Does the index include any words you don't understand and that you would have to look up? List them.
5. Can you think of an insect not covered in the book? Name it.

Ten-Minute Real World Reading ©1997 Monday Morning Books, Inc.

INGREDIENTS LIST

This activity aims to open students' minds to what they put into their open mouths.

DIRECTIONS:
1. Make sure students understand the meaning of the word *ingredient*, something used to make something else. For example, sugar is an ingredient in most cookies.
2. Give each student a copy of the sample Ingredients List, next page.
3. Have students read the ingredients in the box and then answer the questions.
4. Discuss the answers. For your information:
• Gelatin is a tasteless, odorless substance made from either animal bones or vegetables.
• Adipic acid is used as a flavor enhancer.
• Disodium phosphate controls acidity.
• Maltodextrin is a sweetener.
• Fumaric acid is a flavor enhancer and extends shelf life.
• Aspartame is an artificial sweetener
• Acesulfame potassium is a sweetener.
• Salt is a compound that provides one of the four basic flavors.
• Blue 1 and Red 40 are artificial colorings.

EXTENSION:
Have each student choose a manufactured food, and write to the maker for information about the purpose of each ingredient. The manufacturer's address will usually be listed on the package.

Answers for next page:
1. Ten ingredients 2. Disodium phosphate 3. Variable
4. Variable 5. Variable 6. Red 40 adds color to the product.

Sample Ingredients List

Many foods are found in nature. Examples include fresh fruits and vegetables. Other foods are manufactured. This means that they are made of two or more things (ingredients). Examples include ice cream, bread, and cookies.

In many countries, the law says that a package of manufactured food must list the ingredients used to make that food. This way shoppers can find out what they're eating. Lists of ingredients are especially helpful to people who are allergic to specific foods. Ingredient lists are also helpful to concerned eaters who want to know exactly what is in their food before they eat it.

Read the following list of ingredients. Then answer the questions below.

Cherry Gelatin Dessert Mix

GELATIN, ADIPIC ACID, DISODIUM PHOSPHATE, MALTODEXTRIN, FUMARIC ACID, ASPARTAME, ACESULFAME POTASSIUM, SALT, BLUE 1, RED 40

Questions:
1. How many ingredients go into this product?
2. Ingredients are listed in order of quantity. The ingredient that weighs the most, comes first. Which ingredient is the third most by weight?
3. How many ingredients have you <u>not</u> heard of?
4. List each ingredient that you have used yourself.
5. How many of the ingredients listed here have a purpose that you can't figure out from the name?
6. What do you think is the purpose of "Red 40"?

JOKES

Joke-telling is an act that provides practice in memorizing, pacing, and characterization (inventing different voices).

DIRECTIONS:
1. Duplicate and cut apart the Joke Cards, next page. Give one joke to each student.
2. Optional: Keep a joke for yourself and demonstrate an oral interpretation, using two different voices for the characters.
3. Have students read and rehearse their jokes. They should commit them to memory, but it's not necessary to memorize them exactly.
4. Divide the class into pairs and have students share their jokes.

EXTENSION:
Have students find their own jokes to rehearse, and from time to time have a joke-telling session.

Joke Cards

A parent entered a shop and shouted at the clerk, "You charged my son for five pounds of candy, and gave him only three pounds."

"How do you know?"

"I weighed the bag," said the parent.

"Weigh the boy," said the clerk.

One math student asked another, "If I had 10 pears and gave you 2, how many would be left?"

"I don't know," said the other.

"It's easy," said the friend.

"Not for me. In my class, our problems are always about apples."

My best friend was crying the other day. I asked, "What's wrong?"

"I lost my dog," my friend moaned.

"Why don't you put an ad in the newspaper," I suggested.

"That won't help," said my friend. "My dog can't read."

"Hey," shouted my friend, "did you eat all the walnuts?"

"I didn't touch one," I said.

My friend said, "But there's only one left."

I replied, "Yes, that's the one I didn't touch."

"This was the weirdest Halloween ever," said my friend.

"What was so weird about it?" I asked.

"A parrot came to our door."

"What did he do?"

"He shouted, 'Trick or Tweet.'"

"What crop do farmers raise in dry weather?" asked the teacher.

"Peanuts," replied the student.

"What do they raise in wet weather?"

"That's easy. Umbrellas."

LANGUAGE GUIDES

Phonetic spelling provides a shortcut for learning to pronounce phrases is another language.

DIRECTIONS:
1. Divide the class into pairs. Give each pair the Sample Language Guide, next page.
2. Explain that letters often stand for different sounds in different languages. For example, "vous" in French is pronounced "voo." One way to represent the sounds of foreign words is to spell them phonetically.
3. Optional: Demonstrate the dialogue yourself or have an experienced French speaker perform it.
4. Have the students practice the dialogue. Discuss some of the letter patterns that are different in French. For example, the final "t" is not pronounced in words such as *comment*.

EXTENSION:
Repeat the activity using examples from language guides found in the library. If possible, have a native speaker read the phrases on tape or during a classroom visit.

Sample Language Guide - Talking in French

	French spelling	Phonetic spelling	English meaning
Speaker 1	Comment allez-vous?	Kah mah tah lay voo?	How are you?
Speaker 2	Très bien. Et vous?	Tray bee ehn. Ay voo?	Very good. And you?
Speaker 1	Bien, aussi.	Bee ehn, oh see.	Good, also.
Speaker 2	J'ai faim.	Zshay fahm.	I'm hungry.
Speaker 1	Moi, aussi.	Mwah, oh see.	Me, too.
Speaker 2	Est-ce que vous voulez manger?	Es keh voo voo lay mange-ay?	Would you like to eat?
Speaker 1	Oui.	Whee.	Yes.
Speaker 2	Quand?	Kahn?	When?
Speaker 1	Immeditement.	Eh mee dee eh mahn.	Immediately.
Speaker 2	Ou?	Oooh?	Where?
Speaker 1	Aimez-vous Chez Paul?	Ay may voo Shay Paul?	Do you like Paul's Cafe?
Speaker 1	Oui. C'est un bon restaurant.	Whee. Seh tun bohn rest oh rahn.	Yes. It's a good restaurant.
Speaker 2	D'accord.	Dah cor.	Fine.
Speaker 1	Allons-y!	Ah lone zee!	Let's go!

LEASES

Most people have the experience of renting an apartment or home. Carefully examining the lease or rental agreement can make a big difference in terms of having a satisfactory experience.

DIRECTIONS:
1. Explain that a lease is a written agreement between a property owner and someone who wants to use the property for a time. Many kinds of property can be leased including cars, stores, and tools.
2. Give each student, or small group, a copy of the Sample Lease, next page.
3. Have students read the lease and answer the questions.
4. Go over the answers.

EXTENSION:
Challenge students to write a lease for a piece of property they own, for example, a bicycle. Or they could write a lease for a piece of property in a story, for example, the pumpkin coach in *Cinderella*.

Answers for next page:
1. False 2. False 3. False 4. The tenant 5. 1,100 dollars 6. No time

Sample Lease

Read the lease. Then answer the questions below.

Lease

1. Property: This lease covers the use of Apartment 23 in the Oaks Building at 111 Green Avenue. The apartment has five rooms: a living room, a kitchen, two bedrooms, and a bathroom. A refrigerator and a stove are included.

2. Rent: The rent is 1,000 a month. Rent is due on the first day of the month. If the payment is not received by the end of the fifth day of the month, a late charge of 10% will be added.

3. Lease dates: The lease is for one year.

4. Utilities: Rent includes cold and hot water, and heat. The tenant must pay for electricity and telephone.

5. Pets: Only fish, birds, and cats are permitted. No more than two birds and two cats are permitted.

6. Inspection: The owner has the right to inspect the property twice a year, but the owner must give the tenant a week's notice before doing the inspection.

7. Noise: The tenant agrees not to make noise that would disturb neighbors. Practicing a musical instrument is allowed only from 10 a.m. until 6 p.m. No drumming is permitted.

8. Repairs: The owner will make sure the following things work: water heater, refrigerator, plumbing, and elevator.

Questions:
1. True or false: The owner may enter the property whenever the owner chooses.
2. True or false: If the water heater breaks, the tenant must fix it.
3. True or false: The tenant may keep three, four-legged pets.
4. Who pays the bill for electricity used in the apartment?
5. If the rent is paid at noon on the 6th of the month, how much is owed?
6. At what time of the day may a tenant practice playing drums?

LETTERS TO THE EDITOR

The letters column in newspapers and magazines gives an opportunity for exercising freedom of speech. The letters themselves provide material for critical reading.

DIRECTIONS:
1. Make sure students are familiar with the letters column of your local newspaper. Explain that the letters page offers readers a chance to agree or disagree with people who write articles or other letters.
2. Give each student or small group a copy of the sample letter, next page.
3. Have students read the letter and answer the questions.
4. Share the students' responses.

EXTENSION:
Have students write letters in response to material published in your town's newspaper.

Sample Letter to the Editor

Read the following letter. Then do the activities below.

> To the Editor:
> I never saw anything sillier than your article about "E-mail Excitement." What's the big deal about computers and all that other electronic stuff?
> A hundred years ago, no one owned a TV, but people were happy. Maybe they didn't know what was happening on the other side of the world, but why should they? There's always plenty of things to know close to home.
> My friends who use e-mail every day urge me to go "online" so I'll get mail just a few seconds after it's written.
> I tell them, "What's the hurry? Whatever you want to tell me now will be just as interesting next week."
> J. K. Trembleton

Activities:

1. In a sentence or two, describe how the author of "E-mail Excitement" feels about e-mail.

2. Do you think J.K. Trembleton owns a cellular telephone? Why or why not?

3. Do you think the writer would rather live in the past or in the future? Explain your answer in a few sentences.

4. Can you guess how old the letter writer is? If yes, make a guess and give your reason. If no, explain why you can't guess the person's age.

5. Explain why you agree or disagree with this letter.

   Ten-Minute Real World Reading ©1997 Monday Morning Books, Inc.

MENUS

These days, many people eat a large number of meals in restaurants. Part of enjoying this experience is knowing how to make sense of the menu.

DIRECTIONS:
1. Make sure students understand that a menu is a list of choices. The word comes from the French word *minute*, in this sense meaning "little details."
2. Give each student or small group a copy of the Sample Menu, next page.
3. Have students read the menu and then answer the questions.
4. Discuss the answers.

EXTENSION:
Have students collect unusual menus from local restaurants or, by writing letters to friends in other places, from restaurants around the country or around the world. Make a bulletin board display of the menus.

Answers for next page:
1. Vegetarian omelet, Oatmeal and fruit 2. Oatmeal and fruit 3. Hot chocolate 4. You get juice with the Hearty Meal. 5. The savings would be $2.00.

Sample Menu

Look over the menu. Then answer the questions below.

The Daily Diner's Breakfast Menu

Beverages

orange juice	1.00	tea	1.00
grapefruit juice	1.00	coffee	1.00
cranberry juice	1.00	milk	1.00
parsnip juice	1.00	hot chocolate	2.00

Specials

Buttermilk pancakes (4)	4.00
Fruit plate & yogurt	5.00
Ham & 2 eggs	5.00
Hearty Meal (ham, 2 eggs, juice, toast, coffee)	8.00
Vegetarian omelet *	6.00
Waffles and bacon	5.00
Oatmeal and fruit *	3.00
Sunrise Special (ham, 2 eggs, toast, coffee)	7.00

Sides

Toast	2.00	Ham	3.00
Oatmeal	2.00	2 Eggs	3.00
Fruit	2.00	Yogurt	2.00

* Meals marketed with a star have been rated "healthy" by the National Dietary Association.

Questions:
1. List the two special meals that are rated "healthy."
2. What's the least expensive special on the menu?
3. Which costs more: a cup of hot chocolate or a glass of milk?
4. What's the differences between "The Sunrise Special" and "The Hearty Meal"?
5. If you were to order each item in "The Sunrise Special" separately, how much more would it cost you than if you ordered this special?

Ten-Minute Real World Reading ©1997 Monday Morning Books, Inc.

NEWSPAPERS

In the future, news*papers* may be published only digitally, to be read "onscreen." But even such paperless papers will still contain the variety of features that make today's dailies such a rich reading resource.

DIRECTIONS:
1. Divide the class into groups of about five or six.
2. Give each group a copy of a daily newspaper plus the Newspaper Scavenger Hunt, next page.
3. Have students go through the paper, finding examples for each category.
Note: If students are not reading at the level of the newspaper, you could do the activity orally, reading articles and having students identify the categories.

EXTENSION:
Try the same activity with a children's magazine.

Newspaper Scavenger Hunt

Skim a newspaper. List examples that fit the following categories. Some articles might fit more than one category.

CATEGORIES	DEFINITIONS
Advertisements	Pictures and words that sell products.
Advice column	Tips for solving problems or doing tasks.
Business	News about products, trade, money, etc.
Cartoon	A drawing that comments on the news.
Comics	A picture series that tells a story or a joke.
Editorial	An essay giving an opinion.
Government	News about laws or government activities.
History article	A report on a past event.
Human interest	A story about an unusual experience.
Letters to the editor	Opinions sent in by readers of the paper.
Local news	Stories about events close to home.
National news	Stories from places around the country or about the country itself.
News photo	A photograph that tells a story.
Obituaries	Stories about people who recently died.
Puzzle	A word, picture, or number game.
Reviews	Opinions about movies, concerts, and so on.
Science news	Stories about astronomy, medicine, etc.
Sports news	Articles about athletes and teams.
Weather	News about temperature, wind, and storms.
World news	Information about other countries.

 Ten-Minute Real World Reading ©1997 Monday Morning Books, Inc.

ONLINE INTERVIEWS

Interviewing an expert sharpens the skill of asking questions. Conducting an interview online adds the bonus of providing reading practice, as the interviewee's answers appear on the screen.

RESOURCES NEEDED:
• Access to an online computer with software that permits users to engage in a "live" chat.
• An expert willing to be interviewed online.

DIRECTIONS:
1. Ahead of time, set up an online appointment with an expert. Have the students think up questions.
2. To make sure that students understand the format, share the sample interview, next page. Point out the elements:
• The interviewer (labeled "Class" in the sample) asks questions.
• The expert or interviewee ("Scott" in the sample) answers the questions.
3. Sign on, and turn on the "log" or "recording" function so that everything you and the expert type can be printed later.
4. After greeting the expert, have students take turns reading the onscreen text aloud so that the entire class can follow the interview.
5. In addition to asking prepared questions, encourage students to ask additional "follow-up" questions during the interview.
6. After finishing, print the text. Ask one or all of the students to send an e-mail thank-you to the expert.

Sorry, the President is busy giving an e-mail interview to students in Alaska.

OVAL OFFICE

EXTENSION:
Arrange for students in small groups to interview other people. These might include high school students, local citizens, or experts living elsewhere.

Sample Online Interview

2:04 PM: Start log (computer recording)

CLASS: Hi, Scott.

SCOTT: Greetings, good to "see" you.

CLASS: We want to ask you about your life as a fisherman.

SCOTT: Sounds like fun. Where would you like to start?

CLASS: How long were you a fisherman?

SCOTT: Seven years, from 1979 to 1985.

CLASS: Did you take classes to become a fisherman?

SCOTT: No, but I had to "prove" myself as a good worker.

CLASS: What were your jobs on the boat?

SCOTT: Fishing, cooking meals, and navigating.

CLASS: Did you ever get seasick?

SCOTT: At first, I was sick daily. Later, I got used to the motion.

CLASS: Did you consider it a dangerous job?

SCOTT: Most jobs have some risks. Fishing can be dangerous.

CLASS: What were the good points of a fishing job?

SCOTT: Lots of fresh air, good pay, and a sense of freedom.

CLASS: What were the bad points?

SCOTT: Being away from home, bad weather, and long hours.

CLASS: Did you eat fish while you were on the boat?

SCOTT: Not often. That was called "eating your paycheck."

CLASS: Would you recommend the job to someone else?

SCOTT: I liked it, but can't say that everyone would enjoy it.

CLASS: We want to thank you for your time! We learned a lot!

SCOTT: My pleasure.

2:17 PM: Turn off log.

PROVERBS

Proverbs not only offer wisdom. They give readers a chance to interpret metaphoric language.

DIRECTIONS:
1. Write a proverb on the board and ask students to write a few sentences that explain its general meaning. (See example in the margin.)
2. Have students share their ideas in small groups.
3. Discuss their ideas.
4. Optional: Repeat the activity with other proverbs, such as:
• You can't judge a book by its cover.
• Half a loaf is better than none.
• All sunshine makes a desert.

EXTENSION:
Write two related proverbs on the board. For samples, use groups 1-6 on the next page. Have students, alone or with partners explain the link.
(See the example in the margin.)

For a variation, list three proverbs, two related and one unrelated, such as groups 7 and 8. Have students find the proverb that doesn't belong and explain why.

Explaining a Single Proverb
"A bird in the hand equals two in the bush" is really about not being greedy. It means that you might be better off with something that you actually have rather than counting on something that you don't have and might not get.

Comparing Proverbs
• Rome was not built in a day.
• Mighty oaks from little acorns grow.

These two proverbs have the same message. The one about Rome says that it took a long time to build that big city. The second says it takes a long time for a magnificent tree to grow. Both proverbs tell the reader that patience is important. This is especially true if you're trying to accomplish something big.

A small hole can sink a big ship.

Proverbs to Compare

Common Link

Group 1.
One rotten apple spoils the barrel.
A chain is only as strong as its weakest link.

A group depends
on each member.

Group 2.
Don't bite off more than you can chew.
Don't count your chickens before they hatch.

Stay focused on
the present.

Group 3.
No use crying over spilled milk.
Don't make a mountain out of a molehill.

Work on problems
that can be solved.

Group 4.
A stitch in time saves nine.
A small hole can sink a large ship.

Solve small problems
before they get big.

Group 5.
The leopard can't change his spots.
Wood may remain ten years in the water, but
will never become a crocodile.

Our characters are partly
determined
by birth.

Group 6.
To make an omelet, you must break some eggs.
You can't have your cake and eat it too.

Everything has a cost.

Group 7.
A. If you play with fire, you may get burned.
B. He who can't dance will say, "The drum is bad."
C. You reap what you sow.

A and C are about taking
responsibility.
B is about finding
excuses.

Group 8.
A. Talk does not cook rice.
B. Slow and steady wins the race.
C. When in Rome, do as the Romans do.

A and B are about
the importance of
action. C is about
getting along with people.

     Ten-Minute Real World Reading ©1997 Monday Morning Books, Inc.

READERS' THEATER

Readers' Theater is a simple but highly entertaining activity. It puts the emphasis on reading for meaning.

DIRECTIONS:
1. Explain that Readers' Theater is a form of drama in which the actors read their parts. Listeners use imagination to "see" the action.
2. Duplicate a copy of the sample readers' theater script, next five pages, for each actor.
3. Make "audience response cards" (listed in the margin), and give them to the actor playing the Warm-up Person. *Note:* You might want to divide the class into groups, and have each group read the script for themselves.
4. Assign each part to an actor.
5. Have students read the play.

<table>
<tr><td>Audience Response Cards
Applaud.
Laugh.
Hold your breath.
Breathe.
Hiss.
Oooooh.</td></tr>
</table>

EXTENSION:
Put on this play, or other readers' theater dramas, for classes throughout your school. You might also tape it for parents to listen to at home.

Our mystery guest has come millions of miles to be here.

Fifty Million Eyes

CAST:

Warm-up Person · Last Laugh
Chatter Box · Song Bird
Sound-effects Person · Announcer
Kloogy Juxta · Robot
Salesperson

PROP: bell or other noise maker

If there's no audience, all actors play the audience.

WARM-UP PERSON: Our TV program will begin in a moment, but first let's play a game. I'll hold up a few signs. You do what each one says. (Hold up "Applaud" card.)

AUDIENCE: (Clap your hands.)

WARM-UP PERSON: Now do this. (Hold up "Laugh" card.)

AUDIENCE: (Laugh.)

WARM-UP PERSON: I always wanted to be a comedian. Here's one more. (Hold up "Hold your breath" card.)

AUDIENCE: (Hold your breath.)

WARM-UP PERSON: Hm. I'm missing the last card. It's here somewhere.

AUDIENCE: (Groan as if about to explode.)

WARM-UP PERSON: Got it. (Hold up "Breathe" card.)

AUDIENCE: (Make a gasping sound.)

WARM-UP PERSON: The studio clock tells me we're about to go on the air. Five. Four. Three. Two. One.

SOUND EFFECTS PERSON: (Ring a bell.)

ANNOUNCER: "TV Talk" is on the air. Now here's our host, the amazing, the one, the only, Chatter Box.

WARM-UP PERSON: (Hold up "Applaud" card.)

AUDIENCE: (Applaud.)

CHATTER BOX: Thank you, audience and viewers at home. We have a fabulous, once-in-a-lifetime show, just like yesterday's. Our mystery guest has come millions of miles to be here. But first, we have a friend making her fiftieth appearance. Let's hear it for "SONG BIRD."

WARM-UP PERSON: (Hold up "Applaud" card.)

AUDIENCE: (Applaud.)

SONG BIRD: I'd like to do a song that I just learned.
    Twinkle, twinkle, little star,
    How I wonder what you are,
    Up above the world so high,
    Like a diamond in the sky.
    Twinkle, twinkle, little star,
    How I wonder what you are.

WARM-UP PERSON: (Hold up "Applaud" card.)

AUDIENCE: (Applaud.)

CHATTER BOX: That's enough. Now welcome the world's funniest comedian. Someone who needs no introduction.

SONG BIRD: Then stop the introduction.

CHATTER BOX: It's Last-Laugh-Lagoo!

WARM-UP PERSON: (Hold up "Applaud" card.)

AUDIENCE: (Applaud.)

LAST LAUGH: You're a great audience, much better than my family. They won't listen to my jokes. They're so mean.

AUDIENCE: (all together): How mean are they?

LAST LAUGH: They're so mean that they make me listen to *their* jokes.

AUDIENCE: Awwww.

LAST LAUGH: Yesterday, my son told me how strict they are in his school. Whenever he has a question, he has to raise his hand. When I went to school, we weren't even allowed to have questions. You wouldn't believe how strict they were.

AUDIENCE: Tell us anyway.

LAST LAUGH: When we took tests, our eyes had to be glued to the paper. One year I used three bottles of glue. Talk about a strict dress code! We all wore the same uniform. It isn't easy getting 35 kids into one uniform.

AUDIENCE: Yuck.

LAST LAUGH: You want strict? During vacation, our principal relaxed by working as a lion tamer. Only one thing scared our principal—my teacher. She was always getting after me. I don't know why. For example, one day she asked where the Atlantic Ocean was. I told her it was right where it had always been.

WARM-UP PERSON: (Holds up "Applaud.")

AUDIENCE: (Applaud.)

CHATTER BOX: We'll be back after this message.

ANNOUNCER: Try "Memory," the fruit juice that helps you remember. I use it to remember...er...well... I can't recall what, but it's terrific. Just look for the pink... or is it yellow... bottle...maybe can...of...what-cha-ma-call-it.

CHATTER BOX: Our next guest, Kloogy Juxta, has come all the way from the distant planet Kryptogram.

WARM-UP PERSON: (Hold up "Oooooh" card.)

AUDIENCE: (Make an "ooooh" sound.)

CHATTER BOX: Kloogy, tell us about your planet.

KLOOGY: Our air smells like rotten eggs mixed with skunk juice.

CHATTER BOX: Sounds nice. So what brings you here?

KLOOGY: Kryptogramians are going to take over Earth.

CHATTER BOX: You mean an invasion?

KLOOGY: Exactly. So what do you think of that?

CHATTER BOX: It's exciting, especially because you announced it on my show. We'll want to hear all the details of your invasion, right after this brief pause.

ANNOUNCER: Eat Brainoes. It's the only cereal that'll make you smart enough to know how dumb this show is.

CHATTER BOX: Kloogy, when does your invasion begin?

KLOOGY: Tomorrow morning.

LAST LAUGH: Impossible!

KLOOGY: Not with our amazing powers, like ESP.

LAST LAUGH: I don't believe it.

KLOOGY: I knew you were going to say that. But let me prove it. Think of any number you like.

LAST LAUGH: Got it.

KLOOGY: It's 25,313,461 and a half.

LAST LAUGH: Yes, but that was just a lucky guess.

KLOOGY: We have powerful robots that appear at the snap of a thumb. (Snap thumb.)

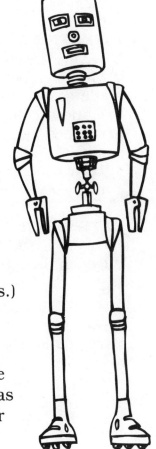

ROBOT: Hi, I'm a powerful robot. I can knock over skyscrapers just by blowing on them. I can move mountains with a single kick.

KLOOGY: So you see, Earthlings are doomed.

CHATTER BOX: This is fabulous. My twenty-five million viewers are grateful that you told them first.

KLOOGY: Twenty-five million viewers? Did you say twenty-five million? I think... I'm going...to faint. (Faints.)

CHATTER BOX: He fainted. But why?

ROBOT: Kryptogramians hate crowds. In fact, their one weakness is stage fright. When Kloogy heard that he was being watched by twenty-five million people, using their fifty million eyes, he couldn't stand the thought.

CHATTER BOX: Will he recover?

ROBOT: Once I get him back to the privacy of our ship.

CHATTER BOX: Have a safe trip home.

ROBOT: Thank you.

CHATTER BOX: Gee, that was a terrific show. But you know what? We have an even more unusual program planned for tomorrow. See you then.

RESPONSIVE READING

A responsive reading is an interactive performance. The leader reads aloud a passage, and the group responds by reading words that echo or develop the idea. The format can be used to present concepts and facts in all academic areas. In the following examples, subjects include insects (science), syllables (language arts), and the orchestra (music).

DIRECTIONS:
1. Divide the class into three groups.
2. Give members of each group a copy of one of the sample readings found on the next three pages.
3. Optional: Demonstrate how a responsive reading is performed by taking the leader's part with one of the samples, and having members of that group respond.
4. Have each group try their readings, making sure that each child has a chance to play the part of the leader.

EXTENSION:
Have students create their own responsive readings, which they can then perform with classmates.

Australia covers an entire continent.

It is the only continent occupied by a single nation.

Sample Responsive Reading

INSECTS

Leader: All insects have six legs.

Group: No other kinds of animals do.

Leader: Most insects have a four-part life cycle.

Group: First they are eggs. Next, they are worm-like larvae. Third, they are pupae surrounded by a cocoon. Fourth, they are adults.

Leader: Most insects fly.

Group: Some have two wings; others have four wings.

Leader: But some cannot fly.

Group: Fleas are a famous example.

Leader: Insects can be useful to humans.

Group: Bees give us honey and pollinate plants. Silkworms create silk thread.

Leader: But many insects cause problems for humans.

Group: Mosquitoes spread disease. Termites damage wood houses.

Leader: The science of insects is called "entomology."

Group: "Ento" means "insect" and "ology" means "study of."

Leader: So the next time an ant climbs on you, take a good look at it.

Group: You should find it interesting, and you'll be an entomologist.

Sample Responsive Reading

SYLLABLES

Leader: A syllable is a speech sound. It's spoken all at once. Some words have only one syllable.

Group: Three one-syllable words are *sky*, *blue*, and *foot*.

Leader: Many words have two syllables.

Group: *Monkey. Playground. Rocket.*

Leader: Some words have three syllables.

Group: *Elephant. Molasses. September.*

Leader: Most words have four syllables or less, but words can have more than that.

Group: One of the longest English words has 11 syllables: an•ti•dis•es•tab•lish•men• tar•i an• ism.

Leader: A prefix is a syllable that is added to the front of a word. It changes the word's meaning. An example is the prefix "un."

Group: You'll hear it in words like *uneasy*, *unusual*, and *unfriendly*.

Leader: A suffix is a syllable that is added to the end of a word. It also changes the meaning.

Group: An example is the suffix "er." It changes *play* into *player*, and *paint* into *painter*.

Leader: Why should you pay attention to syllables?

Group: You'll have an easier time learning to spell, to pronounce, and to understand words.

Sample Responsive Reading

ORCHESTRA

Leader: An orchestra is a musical group that contains four kinds of instruments.

Group: The four kinds are strings, woodwinds, brass, and percussions.

Leader: The stringed instruments usually carry the melody.

Group: Stringed instruments include violins, violas, cellos, basses, and the harp.

Leader: The woodwinds sometimes carry the melody. They also add a different kind of emotion.

Group: The woodwinds are clarinets, flutes, oboes, and bassoons.

Leader: The brass instruments, also called "wind instruments," add force.

Group: The main brass instruments are trumpets, trombones, and French horns.

Leader: Percussion instruments highlight rhythm.

Group: Percussion instruments are played by striking them. These instruments include drums of various sizes, cymbals, chimes, and bells.

Leader: Sometimes other instruments play in an orchestra.

Group: These include the piano, the organ, the harpsichord, the saxophone, and the human voice.

Leader: All the instruments must play together.

Group: To make sure that happens, a conductor leads the musicians.

Ten-Minute Real World Reading ©1997 Monday Morning Books, Inc.

RULES & REGULATIONS

Learning to read and understand rules is a key skill in getting along. This activity also gives students a chance to think about ways for improving the do's and don'ts encountered in everyday life.

DIRECTIONS:
1. Give each student or small group a copy of the Sample Rules, next page.
2. Have students read the rules and answer the questions.
3. Discuss the answers.

EXTENSION:
Have students collect examples of rules found at school or throughout town. If students find a way to improve a set of rules, encourage them to write to the person in charge explaining their views.

Answers for next page:
1. Yes 2. Yes 3. No 4. You may never enter the garden if you're a visitor. 5. No 6. Open ended

Sample Rules

Read the following rules. Then answer the questions at the bottom of the page.

Rincon Park Rules

1. The park is closed from sundown to sunrise.
2. Smoking is not allowed in the picnic or playground areas.
3. Alcoholic beverages are not allowed in the park.
4. Amplified music is not permitted.
5. Volleyball is allowed only using the permanent net.
6. Dogs must be leashed. Owners must clean up after their dogs.
7. Hard balls may not be thrown or batted.
8. Visitors must not enter the flower garden.
9. Skateboarding and skating are permitted only in the rink at the north end of the park, not on the walkway.
10. Motorized model airplanes may not be flown in the park.
11. To avoid overcrowding, rangers may limit park admission.
12. Use of the cooking grills is by permission only. For a permit, phone the City Parks Department.

Questions:
1. Is it OK to fly a model glider in the park?
2. Is it OK to visit the park during a storm?
3. If rangers stop you from entering the park because they say it's too crowded, can you enter if you don't mind crowds?
4. During what hours may you enter the flower garden?
5. If no one is using a grill, can you use one without getting a permit?
6. Is there any rule that you think should be added, omitted, or changed? Explain your thinking.

Ten-Minute Real World Reading ©1997 Monday Morning Books, Inc.

SCHEDULES

Whether trying to catch a bus heading across the country, or a rocket going to Mars, travelers need to know how to read schedules.

DIRECTIONS:
1. Give each student a copy of the Sample Schedule, next page.
2. Explain that in outer space, as in many parts of the world, time is measured using a 24-hour clock.
    Midnight is 0000. Nine a.m. is 0900. Noon is 1200.
    Three p.m. is 1500.
3. Have students read the schedule and answer the questions.
4. Go over their answers.

EXTENSIONS:
To practice down-to-earth schedule reading, have students collect (or write away for) bus, train, ferry, and plane timetables. Later, students might create their own imaginary schedules, for example, for a time travel company, or for a company that arranges tours of the human body, inspired by Ray Bradbury's novel, *Fantastic Voyage.*

Answers for next page:
1. Sunday at 1800 hours 2. Thursday at 1500 3. Yes
4. The 1800 flight 5. November 1, 2015.

Sample Schedule

Read the schedule. Then answer the questions.

Moon Flight Schedule (beginning November 1, 2015)

	Earth to the Moon							Moon to Earth						
	Sun	Mon	Tues	Wed	Thur	Fri	Sat	Sun	Mon	Tues	Wed	Thur	Fri	Sat
0000														
0100														
0200														
0300												F		
0400														
0500														
0600		A	O							S				
0700														
0800														
0900														
1000														
1100												A		
1200			A											
1300														
1400														
1500				F										
1600									B	A				
1700														
1800	B		A											
1900														
2000														
2100														
2200														
2300														

Symbols:
A: Standard flight: 3 day journey
B: Bargain flight: 1/2 off regular fares
F: High speed flight: takes 2 days instead of 3
O: Orbits the moon but does not land.
S: Flies only in June, July, and August

Questions

1. If you want the cheapest ticket from the Earth to the moon, what day and time must you leave?
2. If you want to get from the Earth to the moon in the shortest time, what day and hour must you leave?
3. Is there a trip to the moon every Wednesday?
4. If you must fly on a Tuesday to attend a meeting on the moon, which flight should you take: the one that leaves at 600 or the one that leaves at 1800?
5. When did this schedule go into effect?

TABLES

Novices sometimes find fact tables intimidating. But that problem is easy to remedy with a little practice.

DIRECTIONS:
1. Ask students a riddle: "What kind of table has no legs, but is often found in libraries?"
2. Give each student a copy of the sample table, next page. Explain that this format, sometimes called a "chart," is a map-like grid used to store facts on a topic, such as weather, sports, minerals, jobs, geography, and so on.
3. Have students read the table and answer the questions.
4. Discuss the answers.

EXTENSION:
Have each student locate and make a report about a table found in an encyclopedia, an almanac, or other book.

I need to know how long the Amazon is.

You're looking for the other kind of table.

Answers for next page:
1. Jupiter is the largest planet; Pluto is the smallest. 2. Mars 3. Pluto is the only other planet. 4. It's because that column gives the distance to Earth. 5. Neptune 6. Open ended, for example, "Planetary Facts."

Sample Table

Read the table. Then answer the questions below. The small, bold numbers refer to the notes in the box.

Planets[1]	Size[2]	Length of year in Earth days[3]	Length of day in Earth hours	Number of moons	Closest distance to Earth in millions of kilometers (miles)
Mercury	8	88	1416	0	80 (50)
Venus	6	225	5,400	0	40 (25)
Earth	5	365	24	1	—
Mars	7	687	25	2	56 (35)
Jupiter	1	4,380	10	16	589 (368)
Saturn	2	10,585	10	17	1192 (745)
Uranus	3	30,660	16	5	2570 (1606)
Neptune	4	60,225	18	2	4267 (2667)
Pluto	9	90,520	154	1	4261 (2663)[4]

Notes:
1. Planets are listed in order from closest to the sun to furthest from the sun.
2. Size rankings (in circumference) are from 1 (largest) to 9 (smallest).
3. A year is the time it takes for the planet to make one trip around the sun.
4. Although Pluto usually is further from earth than Neptune, at its closest point, Pluto comes nearer to Earth than Neptune does.

Questions:
1. Which planet is the largest and which is the smallest?
2. Which planet has a day that is closest to Earth's in length.
3. How many planets have the same number of moons as the Earth?
4. In the last column, why is there no number for Earth?
5. Which planet has the second longest year?
6. If you were to give this table a title, what would it be?

TRAVEL DIRECTIONS

Getting lost isn't fun. But learning how <u>not</u> to get lost can be.

DIRECTIONS:
1. Give each student a copy of the Sample Directions, next page.
2. Have students follow the directions. They should use a pencil to trace a path as they go.
3. Go over the answers.

EXTENSION:
Have students draw maps and give directions for local journeys, for example, from one part of the school to another, or from school to home.

Answers for next page:
1. First Avenue 2. East 3. Whitecalf Road and Torbett Avenue
4. Five blocks 5. One possible shorter route is to take First Avenue straight to the City Park.

Sample Directions

Use the directions to trace a path on the map from the school to the party. Then answer the questions below the map.

Directions to the Party
1. Start at the school.
2. Go three blocks east.
3. Turn right on Brannon Street.
4. Head south to the "T" formed by River Road.
5. Turn left. (You will be going east.) Continue until you reach East Road.
6. Go north on East Road until you reach First Avenue.
7. Enter the park and look for the signs leading to the Old Grove.

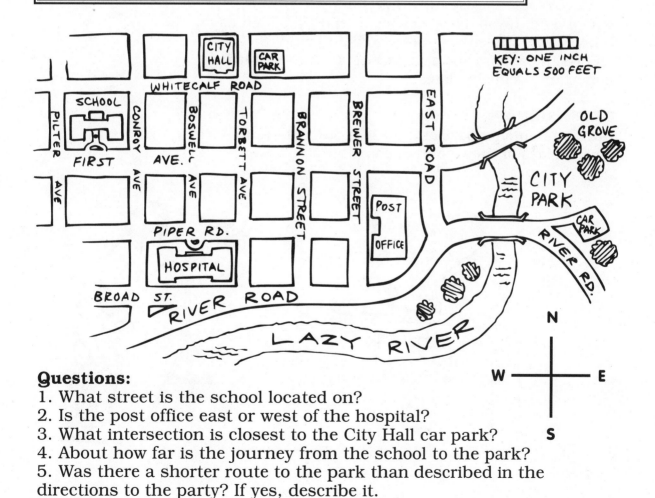

Questions:
1. What street is the school located on?
2. Is the post office east or west of the hospital?
3. What intersection is closest to the City Hall car park?
4. About how far is the journey from the school to the park?
5. Was there a shorter route to the park than described in the directions to the party? If yes, describe it.

Ten-Minute Real World Reading ©1997 Monday Morning Books, Inc.

TV NEWS COPY

In many countries, people who report the news on TV and radio are called "news readers." Their job is to read the news with clarity and meaning.

DIRECTIONS:
1. Divide the class into groups of four to six students.
2. Give each group a copy of the Historic News Reports, next page. Have students cut apart the page so that each reader gets a report. Note that difficult-to-pronounce words are spelled phonetically in brackets.
3. Allow a few minutes for students to rehearse their report. Suggest that they practice looking up from the cards at least once. This will prepare them for making eye contact when they read for an audience.
4. Have readers present the news to their groups.
5. Optional: If you'd like to have a report for each day of the school year, students can research and write their own reports. Most libraries have fact books that highlight important events by date.

EXTENSION:
Have students prepare and present current events "briefs" for the class or the whole school.

Historic News Reports

January 1, 1901
Australia today declared itself to be a commonwealth, consisting of six states. The island continent was first settled thousands of years ago by explorers thought to be from Southeast Asia. Dutch sailors were the first Europeans to visit the area in 1642. In 1770, Captain James Cook landed in Botany Bay and claimed the region for England.

September 15, 1609
This evening, Italian scientist Galileo [pronounced GA LI LAY O] became the first astronomer to study the moon using a telescope. Professor Galileo saw that the moon has many Earth-like features. These include mountains, valleys, and plains. Galileo next plans to study the planet Jupiter, which is the largest planet in the solar system.

August 28, 1963
Martin Luther King, Jr. today addressed several hundred thousand people at a civil rights rally in the heart of Washington, D.C. Reverend King spoke about his hopes for race relations. "I have a dream," he said, "that this nation will rise up and live out the true meaning of its creed...that all men are created equal."

October 12, 1492
After 93 days at sea, Cristophe [KRIS TOFF] Colombo reached an island which he believes is located near China. The Italian sailor, also known as Christopher Columbus, commands three Spanish ships: the Nina, the Pinta, and the Santa Maria. His goal is to open a route between Spain and the Orient. This mission is being paid for by the Spanish royal family.

September 3, 1928
Alexander Fleming today observed a very strange and as yet unexplained event in his laboratory. Dr. Fleming noticed that bacteria which had been growing in a special dish suddenly died. Upon close observation, Dr. Fleming noticed the presence of a mold, known as penicillium [pronounced PEH NI SILL I UM]. Exactly how the mold kills the bacteria remains to be investigated.

December 3, 1967
In Cape Town, South Africa, Dr. Barnard and 30 assistants completed the first human heart transplant operation giving Louis Washkansky [pronounced WASH KAN SKEE] the heart of Denise Darvall. Dr. Barnard later said, "The moment when it all really hit me was just after I had taken out Washkansky's heart. I looked down and saw this empty space."

Ten-Minute Real World Reading ©1997 Monday Morning Books, Inc.

FICTION: CHARACTERS

Characterization involves much more than physical details. Experienced readers look for a variety of clues in order to understand a story's characters.

DIRECTIONS:
1. Explain that characterization means creating a character. This may involve:
• physical description
• habits and revealing actions
• dialogue about the character
• the character's own words and thoughts
2. Give each student a copy of the Getting to Know a Character handout, next page.
3. Have students read the story and answer the questions.
4. Discuss the answers.

EXTENSION:
Ask students to write character-focused book reports. Each essay should cover two or more techniques that the author used to create three-dimensional characters. Later, students might use the techniques in their own fiction.

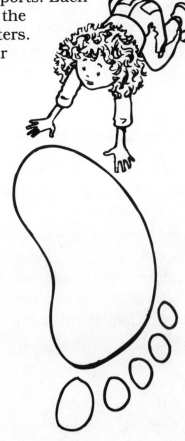

Answers for next page:
1. Arachne had "dusty brown hair" and wore "plain country clothes."
2. Arachne says that Athena is "afraid."
3. Arachne's fingers "trembled," showing that she was nervous.
4. Arachne called herself "the best."

Getting to Know a Character

Read the story. Then follow the directions below.

The Best

People came from all over Greece to see Arachne. It wasn't because she was pretty. Few visitors even noticed her dusty brown hair or plain country clothes. They came to see Arachne weave.

Her quick fingers sent the shuttle moving so fast, it was a blur. Almost like magic, the colorful threads turned into designs that were more beautiful than those made by any other human. When asked how she learned her craft, she bragged, "I taught myself."

One day, an old woman stepped from the onlookers and said to Arachne, "I heard that the goddess Athena taught you to weave. Why don't you give her any credit?"

Arachne said, "I owe her nothing. I'd like a chance to show her that I am the best. But she's afraid to compete with me."

Suddenly, the old woman changed into the beautiful goddess Athena. "Let's see who's the best," said the goddess.

Two looms were set up and the contest began. Arachne's fingers trembled. Still, she wove a magnificent picture. But when Athena finished, everyone knew that her work was better than Arachne's.

Athena tore Arachne's weaving to pieces, and then turned Arachne into a spider. Then she told the young woman, "You lied and bragged. From now on, you and your offspring will weave only one thing: webs for catching insects."

Find the following character descriptions:
1. A physical detail about how a character looks.
2. A comment that one character makes about another.
3. An action that shows what a character is thinking or feeling.
4. A character's self-description.

FICTION: DIALOGUE

Dialogue isn't just talk. It's a tool that writers use to move a story along. In this activity, students learn the four major uses of dialogue.

DIRECTIONS:

1. Make sure that students understand the basics of dialogue:
- Dialogue is what characters say.
- Each piece of dialogue is called a speech.
- Dialogue is set off from the description (the narration) by quotation marks.
- A dialogue tag tells who is talking and how the words are spoken (He said; She shouted; I whispered).
- Usually, a new speech is placed in its own paragraph.

2. Give each student a copy of the Dialogue Hunt handout, next page.

3. Have students read the story and answer the questions.

4. Discuss the answers.

EXTENSION:

In a story or novel, have students find examples of the major uses of dialogue. These include:
- Describing an action, object, or character: "You're eating too fast."
- Revealing an emotion: "I've never been happier."
- Commanding or arguing: "Give me that thing!"
- Asking or answering: "Where do you think you're going?" "None of your business."

Answers for next page:
1. Six 2. "This is fun!" "I'm falling!" and "Never!" 3. "You're flying too high." "There's the Greek coast in the distance." 4. One reason is that he felt his invention was too dangerous.

Dialogue Hunt

Read the story, then answer the questions below.

Daedelus and Icarus

Long ago, on the Greek island of Crete, lived Daedelus, a famous builder. After constructing a palace for King Minos, Daedelus told the king, "My son Icarus and I want to leave the island."

Minos replied, "No. You're too important to me. You must stay."

Later, while watching birds, Daedelus got an idea. He and his son gathered feathers. Using wax, Daedelus attached the feathers to wood frames. After much work, he created two pairs of wings.

The father and son put on the wings. From a tower, they leaped into the air and flew toward Greece. Daedelus warned Icarus, "Do not go too high or the sun's heat will melt the wax."

Ignoring his father, Icarus flew higher. "What a view!" he shouted. "There's the Greek coast in the distance."

Daedelus repeated his warning, but his son wouldn't listen.
Soon the boy was so high, the sun warmed the wax. The feathers began to come off. By the time Icarus saw what was happening, his wings no longer worked.

"I'm falling!" he shouted. He crashed into the sea and drowned.

In tears, Daedelus flew on until he reached land. When people saw his flying invention, they asked him to make wings for them. Daedelus answered with a single word: "Never!"

Questions:
1. How many speeches are there in the story?
2. Which speech or speeches show strong emotion?
3. Which speeches tell what a character sees?
4. Why did Daedelus answer "Never!" at the end of the story?

Ten-Minute Real World Reading ©1997 Monday Morning Books, Inc.

FICTION: GENRES

Each genre—fantasy, mystery, and so on—features a unique set of conventions. That's why genre awareness helps prepare readers to get the most from a given piece of fiction.

DIRECTIONS:
1. Explain that stories can be placed in categories by their central actions and settings. The categories are called genres. For example, a Civil War novel fits in the historical fiction genre.
2. Give each student a copy of the Genre Match handout, next page.
3. Have students match each story synopsis with a type of genre.
4. Go over the answers.

Note: Some stories fit into more than one genre.

EXTENSION:
To broaden their reading range, encourage students to read and report on books from a few genres that they had not read before. For example, someone who reads only science fiction might try a mystery novel and a western. A related activity would be to write movie reviews focusing on different genres.

Answers for next page:
1. H   2. I   3. A, F   4. D, G   5. I
6. C   7. J   8 . B, F, J   9. E   10. D

Genre Match

Ten genres are described on the left. Find an example of each from the list on the right. Some stories match more than one genre. Write the matches on your own paper.

Genres

1. Action: This kind of story is filled with chases, fights, and other exciting happenings.

2. Animal story: The action focuses on one or more animals that act like animals.

3. Fantasy: Animals and objects behave in ways that never happen in real life.

4. Historical Fiction: The action is set in the past.

5. Journey: Characters move from place to place. This is sometimes called a "road story."

6. Mystery (or "whodunit"): A hero tries to figure out who committed a crime.

7. Love story: The action focuses on a relationship.

8. Science fiction: The story involves realistic events that might happen in the future.

9. Sports: The action focuses on an athlete or team.

10. Western: The action takes place in the western United States in the 19th century.

Examples

A. Two talking cats teach a mouse how to talk.

B. Three kids build a time machine out of an old car and a computer, and visit the future.

C. A teacher, helped by her student, finds the thief who has been stealing library books.

D. Two Mexican families defend their ranches in California just before the discovery of gold.

E. A very short kid tries to become a star basketball player.

F. A robot becomes a movie star.

G. An orphan from England settles in Australia at the start of the nineteenth century.

H. Two groups of undersea treasure hunters fight over a sunken ship.

I. A lost dog travels across the country in search of its home.

J. A time traveler from the future falls in love with her host who lives in the present time.

FICTION: MOTIVATION

Just as clever detectives look for motives, smart readers must figure out what makes each character tick.

DIRECTIONS:
1. Ask each student to choose a major character from a story read in class or independently.
2. Students should identify one important act that the character does. For example, the father in *Rumpelstiltskin* brags that his daughter can spin straw into gold.
3. Have each student write a short essay that explains why the character took the action. This could be written from the character's point of view. See a sample on the next page.
4. Have students share their work in small groups.

EXTENSION:
Have students write about the motives of real people found in history, current events, or their own lives.

Classic Motives
ambition
charity
envy
fame
fear
friendship
greed
jealousy
laziness
love
obedience
pride
revenge
values

Why I Built My House Out of Straw

Sample Motivation Essay

Why I Talked to the Wolf
by Little Red Riding Hood

Some people wonder why I spent so much time talking to the wolf when I entered my grandmother's cottage. You remember, I said things like "Oh, Grandmother, what big ears you have." I know that if most people saw a big wolf in their grandmother's bed, they'd scream or run away.

I didn't run away because I wasn't sure what was going on. I thought maybe Grandmother was playing a joke on me. If I ran away, it could make her upset.

I also thought, maybe this isn't my grandmother wearing a disguise. Maybe it really is the wolf. But if I turned and ran, the wolf could jump out of bed and get me. Keeping the wolf talking, if it were the wolf, could give me time to figure out a plan.

My plan worked for a while. Unfortunately, I made a mistake when I said, "Oh, Grandma, what big teeth you have." Hearing the word "teeth" reminded the wolf about eating me up. If I ever find myself in the same predicament, I think I'll ask about his tail or his toes.

Ten-Minute Real World Reading ©1997 Monday Morning Books, Inc.

FICTION: PLOT

The plot gives a story its structure. Learning to recognize the important elements in a plot—the "plot points"—enables students to read fiction at a deeper level.

DIRECTIONS:
1. Have each student choose a familiar story, or choose one that the whole class knows, perhaps a story that you've recently read aloud.
2. Make sure students understand the meaning of plot: the important actions that create the structure (skeleton) of a story.
3. Give each student or small group a copy of the Plot Points handout, next page.
4. Have them find each point in the story that they chose.

EXTENSION:
Have students use the Plot Points handout as a guide for a report that analyzes the plot of a novel.

Plot Points

The plot is what happens in a story. There are many different plots, but most contain the following six parts, called plot points.

1. Set-up: The first part of the plot introduces us to the main character, also called the "protagonist." We see his or her world. Usually, things are going smoothly. For example, the set-up in "Little Red Riding Hood" shows the protagonist preparing goodies for her grandmother.

2. Trigger event: Something out of the ordinary happens to the main character. This pushes the protagonist in a new direction or takes him or her into a different world. For example, in *The Wizard of Oz*, the tornado carries Dorothy to Oz.

3. Problem: The trigger event creates a problem that the main character must face, or a goal that the character wants to reach. Often, at this point in the story, a choice must be made that raises a question, for example, will Goldilocks enter the bears' house or not?

4. Struggle: Now, something comes along that blocks the main character from easily finding the solution or reaching the goal. This opposing force may take the form of a character (the antagonist or villain). But sometimes the block comes from nature, for example, a flood. It can even come from inside the protagonist, for example, a fear of heights.

5. Climax: At this point in the story, we learn how the struggle turns out. If the protagonist solves the problem or reaches the goal, the story has a happy ending. If the goal isn't reached, usually the protagonist learns something important about life.

6. Anticlimax: Here, all of the loose ends of the plot are tied together. Usually, the main character's life is back to normal. Things may be different now than they were at the start of the story, but calm has returned.

 Ten-Minute Real World Reading ©1997 Monday Morning Books, Inc.

FICTION: POINT OF VIEW

Every story involves a storyteller, a subject, and an audience. How these parts fit together determines the story's point of view.

DIRECTIONS:
1. Make sure students understand that most stories are written using one of the three major points of view:
• First person uses the pronouns *I* (first person singular) or *we* (first person plural).
• Second person (found mainly in advertisements and directions) uses the pronoun *you*.
• Third person uses the pronouns *he*, *she*, *it*, or *they*.
2. Give each student a copy of the Point of View worksheet, next page.
3. Have students read and label each story according to its point of view.
4. Go over the answers in class.

EXTENSION:
Have students rewrite one of the stories using a different point of view, for example, switching from first person to third person.

It's the first day of your vacation, and already you're bored. You try to think of something to do, but your mind is a blank.

Answers for next page:
1. B   2. C   3. D   4. A

Point of View

Read each of the paragraphs. Then answer the questions below.

A. The small rabbit raced across the garden and then froze like a statue. His ears pointed toward the sky. He was so still that for a moment it seemed as if he were no longer alive.

B. I looked through the telescope and couldn't believe my eyes. No one had ever seen this sight before. I should have been excited about the discovery, but in fact I was scared.

C. The day was hot and windy. We knew we had to keep moving, but none of us had much energy left. It felt as if we had been walking for weeks, although this was only the third day of our journey.

D. You can't believe it, can you? As you stare through the small round window, you know that you're looking at the moon. In a few hours, you'll be landing there and then moving across the surface in a strange-looking moon buggy. You know all this, and yet it seems absolutely impossible.

Questions:
1. Which example is told in the first person singular?
2. Which example is told in the first person plural?
3. Which example is told in the second person?
4. Which example is told in the third person?

FICTION: SCENES

Scenes are the building blocks of stories. Asking students to identify and think about scenes will help them gain a firmer grasp of story structure.

DIRECTIONS:
1. Make sure students understand what a scene is: an action that happens in one place at one time.
2. Give each student a copy of the Scene Study handout, next page.
3. After students answer the questions, discuss their answers.
4. Optional: Have students share the new scenes that they created for the story.

EXTENSION:
Try scene-focused book reports. You might suggest that students discuss a specific number of scenes, for example, the novel's five most important scenes.

| **Answers for next page:** |
| 1. Three scenes   2. The first and third scene   3. Open ended |

Scene Study

Read the following story. Then answer the questions below.

The Lion and the Mouse

One afternoon, a lion was napping by the river when something tickled him. It was a mouse sitting on his nose.

"You woke the king of the jungle!" roared the lion. "For that, I'll have to eat you up."

"If you let me go," said the mouse, "I'll help you some day."

The lion laughed loudly. "How could a small creature like you help a mighty beast like me? You are too silly to devour." With that, the lion let the mouse go and returned to sleep.

At home, the mouse told her family what had happened. Like the lion, they didn't think she could help a huge beast.

A few weeks later, the mouse was walking near the river again when she heard a roar. She looked around and saw trappers tying the lion with rope.

The day was hot, so the trappers decided to nap before carrying the lion to the zoo. As soon as they started snoring, the mouse tiptoed toward the lion.

"Have you come to make fun of me?" asked the lion.

The mouse said nothing, but started gnawing on the ropes. In a few minutes, she freed the king of the forest. The lion humbly thanked her. He then went off to tell all the other animals that real friendship has nothing to do with size.

Questions:
1. How many scenes does the story have?
2. Which scenes happen in one place but at different times?
3. What might be the next scene if the story were to continue?

FICTION: SETTINGS

Stories can carry us from here to the ends of the world . . . and beyond. Part of the joy of reading is visiting different times and different places.

DIRECTIONS:
1. Explain that setting includes both the place and the time of a story. For example, in a science fiction story, the setting might be "Ottawa in the year 2075." Point out that most stories have more than one setting.
2. Give students the Story Settings handout, next page. Have students read the three stories and answers the questions.
3. Go over the answers in class.

EXTENSION:
In a book report, have students focus on the setting or the settings of the story. For a greater challenge, students can compare the settings in two books.

Where **AM** I?

Story Settings

Read the following stories. Then answer the questions.

A. Two Hikers

Two hikers met in a forest. They promised to help each other if they should encounter any problem.

Suddenly, a bear rushed them. One hiker escaped up a tree. "Help," said his companion. "I don't know how to climb."

"Help yourself," said the man who was up the tree.

The hiker who couldn't climb suddenly remembered that bears prefer live food. He fell down, pretending to be dead. The bear sniffed at the hiker's head and then left.

The man in the tree climbed down and asked, "What did the bear whisper into your ear?"

"He told me that I was foolish traveling with a coward."

B. The Porcupine and the Snakes

One cold winter day, a porcupine was walking along and came upon a cave in which a family of friendly snakes lived.

"Snakes," said the porcupine, "please let me in. It's freezing out here."

The snakes immediately invited the porcupine to join them.

"It's so warm and pleasant in here," said the porcupine.

However, the snakes soon discovered that the porcupine's quills were jabbing them.

"Could you please leave the cave?" said one of the snakes. "We can't sleep with you in here."

"Absolutely not," said the porcupine. "If you don't like it, you leave."

C. Two Rabbits

Two rabbits were fighting about which had smoother fur. They made so much noise, they attracted the attention of a huge, hungry bird who flew down and grabbed them both.

Questions:
1. In which story does time play an important part?
2. In which story is the setting not very important?
3. Which story has two settings?
4. In Story A, what thing in the setting does a character use?

FICTION: THEME

Successful readers know how to discover and articulate
the main lesson of a story.

DIRECTIONS:
1. Make sure students understand that "theme" means the
lesson taught by a story. Point out that a story can have
more than one theme, and that different readers might learn
different lessons from the same story.
2. Give each student a copy of the Understanding Theme
handout, next page.
3. Have students read the fable and answer the questions.
4. Discuss the answers. Because theme involves
interpretation, there will be more than one right answer.
What's important is that students be able to defend their
choices with logical reasoning.

EXTENSION:
Repeat the activity using other fables presented in the
Resources section of this book, or have students do "theme
book reports" in which they focus on one or more lessons in
the books they read.

Understanding Theme

Read the following fable. Then answer the questions below.

A Fable

A shepherd kept his sheep in a field at the edge of town. One day, when he was bored, he shouted out, "The wolf is here. He's going to eat my sheep. Help!"

All the villagers came running. But when they got to the field, they saw no wolf. The shepherd said, "He ran away."

After the villagers returned to their work, the shepherd said to himself, "That was fun getting everyone to run here. I'll try it again."

He shouted, "The wolf is back! The wolf back!"

Once more, the people hurried to the field. Once more, they found no wolf and began to grumble.

An hour later, the shepherd noticed that a huge wolf was coming toward the field. The shepherd screamed, "Help me, everyone, the wolf is here! This time he really is here."

But no one came, and the wolf got fat eating up the sheep.

Questions:

1. Choose one of the following titles for this story or write your own. Briefly tell why you think it's a good title for the story.
   - A. The Shepherd
   - B. The Wolf
   - C. The Lie
   - D. The Silly Villagers

2. The theme is a story's lesson. Which sentence below best sums up the theme of the story? If you like, write your own theme.
   - A. Don't take a job that bores you.
   - B. Don't lie to people who might help you some day.
   - C. If you're going to fool people, do it only once.
   - D. When people call for help, don't believe them.

3. Explain how this theme relates to everyday life.

 Ten-Minute Real World Reading ©1997 Monday Morning Books, Inc.

SKILL: COMPARING

Comparing two pieces of writing provides practice in higher-level thinking skills. The items to compare might be two poems, two short stories, two novels, two nonfiction books, or any similar works.

DIRECTIONS:
1. Read aloud two picture books that relate in at least one way. They might have the same type of protagonist, antagonist, theme, plot, or setting. For example, *The True Story of the 3 Little Pigs* and *Alexander and the Terrible, No Good, Very Bad Day* both feature characters who feel picked on. See the next page for additional pairs.
2. Using a Venn diagram or a grid, have the class help you sort out the books' similarities and differences.
3. If time permits, have students write a paragraph that sums up the books' similarities and differences. The paragraph might include a sentence that explains why one book is better than the other.

EXTENSION:
Students can use the same method to write book reports that compare two nonfiction books (for example, two books about the moon), two novels on the same theme, or a novel and a movie based on that novel.

Works to Compare

Picture Books

The Little Engine That Could & *The Little House*: self-awareness
The Tale of Peter Rabbit & *Where the Wild Things Are*: adventure
The Red Balloon & *Stevie*: loss
The Cat in the Hat & *Curious George*: responsibility
Horton Hatches the Egg & *William's Doll*: integrity
There's a Nightmare in My Closet & *The Island of the Skog*: courage

Novels to Compare

Alice's Adventures in Wonderland & *The Wonderful Wizard of Oz*: journeys
    to strange worlds
Charlotte's Web & *Tuck Everlasting*: friendship
The Lion, the Witch, and the Wardrobe & *The Dark Is Rising*: good vs. evil
The Adventures of Pinocchio & *Tales of a Fourth Grade Nothing*: growing up
Charlie and the Chocolate Factory & *James and the Giant Peach*: adventure

Books Made into Movies

The Adventures of Pinocchio
Alice's Adventures in Wonderland
The Black Stallion
Charlie and the Chocolate Factory
Charlotte's Web
The Grinch Who Stole Christmas
James and the Giant Peach
Jungle Book
The Little Prince
The Lorax
Mrs. Frisbee and the Rats of NIMH
Old Yeller
One Hundred and One Dalmatians
The Outsiders
Phantom Toll Booth
Ramona
The Red Balloon
Sarah, Plain and Tall
The Secret Garden
Twenty Thousand Leagues Under the Sea
Watership Down
The Wonderful Wizard of Oz

SKILL: PARAPHRASING

If done mindfully, paraphrasing can be a powerful tool for mastering material. The following strategies help students understand the process by paraphrasing for a specific purpose.

DIRECTIONS:
1. Explain that paraphrasing means putting ideas into the reader's own words. This involves thinking about the meaning <u>before</u> writing anything. One trick is to read a passage, then write a new version of it without looking at the original words.
2. Have students read a short passage, such as those found on the next page.
3. Ask students to paraphrase the material in a way that simplifies it, so that young children could understand it. This task may involve:
• replacing difficult words with more familiar words
• breaking long sentences into two or more shorter sentences with simpler structures
• adding examples to make abstract ideas concrete
4. Have students share their paraphrases in small groups and compare the results.

EXTENSION:
Try having students paraphrase with the goal of shortening (abridging) a text, for example, by 50 percent.

Sample Passages to Paraphrase

The History of Miniature Golf

By the 1920s, golf was a popular pastime among wealthy people. However, the great majority of people did not have the opportunity to participate in the game.

This inspired John Carter to invent a new variation of the game. His idea was to play golf in a small area and to limit the strokes to putting. He called the new pastime "Tom Thumb" golf in honor of a diminutive circus performer whose height was about three feet (one meter).

Although the original name was soon dropped, the game became popular as miniature golf.

A Lucky Accident

In the old days, wheels were made of wood. Many people realized that rubber wheels would smooth the ride on bicycles and in other vehicles. But there was a problem. When rubber got hot, it became sticky. When it got cold, it became brittle.

In the 1830s, Charles Goodyear sought a solution. He mixed raw rubber with many things, but his experiments failed.

Then one day, Goodyear accidentally dropped a piece of rubber mixed with sulfur onto a hot stove. Instead of melting, it became tough and yet remained flexible. Goodyear realized that "cooking" the rubber with sulfur made it useful. Recalling the Roman fire god Vulcan, he named his method "vulcanization."

Grass

There are more than 10,000 kinds of grass. Some are less than an inch (3 centimeters) tall. Others, such as bamboo, grow to twice the height of a human being.

All members of the grass family have straight, pointy leaves. Many have hollow stems. Like many plants, grasses have flowers, but grass flowers are generally easy to overlook. They are usually pollinated by the wind rather than by insects. The kind of grasses found in ordinary lawns have short stems that are undamaged by cutting. They re-grow from the base of the stem. The flowers, while small, put out enormous quantities of pollen, which is an important cause of hay fever.

 Ten-Minute Real World Reading ©1997 Monday Morning Books, Inc.

SKILL: PREDICTING

Savvy readers try to anticipate where a writer is leading. Whether the prediction is right or wrong, simply looking ahead increases involvement in the material.

DIRECTIONS:
1. Read aloud the title of a short article. In addition to those on the next page, you could use articles found in magazines and newspapers.
2. Have students list several topics that the article might be about.
3. Optional: Read the first line of the article. Again, have students predict what the article will cover.
4. Read the rest of the article and discuss the students' predictions.

EXTENSION:
Have students write "prediction" book reports. After finishing each chapter, they should write a paragraph predicting what the next chapter will be about. The book report will consist of the series of predictions.

Prediction Practices

In the Wrong Place
A weed is any plant that grows where it isn't wanted.
For example, grass is a weed when it grows in a
vegetable garden. A tomato plant would be a weed if it
came up in the middle of a golf course. Most people
think of dandelions as weeds. But for people who enjoy
eating dandelion leaves in a salad, dandelions are a
valued vegetable.

Eyes in the Back of the Head?
Have you ever tried to sneak up on a rabbit?
Good luck. Usually, the rabbit will hop about without
turning around. It's almost as if the rabbit has extra
eyes back there. In truth, rabbits have two eyes just
like people. But because their eyes stick out from each
side of the head, rabbits can see nearly in a full circle.
Deer and other animals that are hunted have the same
kind of eyes.

A Living, Breathing Helicopter
The tiny hummingbird has flying abilities that match
the most advanced helicopters. Like a helicopter, a
hummingbird can hover in one place, move straight
up and straight down, dart to the side, and even fly
backwards. Part of the trick is the bird's ability to flap
its wings 75 times a second. Equally important, the
hummingbird can rotate the angle of its wings. This
means that it can push the air in many directions.

What's the Largest Fish?
The whale is the largest creature in history, bigger by
far than the biggest dinosaurs, but it isn't a fish. Whales
have lungs, just like humans, whereas fish breathe
through gills. The biggest fish is the whale shark, which
measures about 60 feet (20 meters).

 Ten-Minute Real World Reading ©1997 Monday Morning Books, Inc.

SKILL: PRE-READING

One way to increase reading speed and efficiency is deciding which books to read in the first place. Efficient readers know the tricks for getting a quick feel for a book's contents and "personality."

DIRECTIONS:
1. Ahead of time, collect a dozen or more short nonfiction books from a children's library. Or have students bring in such books.
2. If students aren't familiar with the parts of a book, give them a sample tour. Cover the elements listed in the Pre-Reading Guide, next page.
3. Divide the class into small groups. Make sure each group has a book and a copy of the Pre-Reading Guide.
4. Have the groups go through their books and answer the questions on the checklist. If a book doesn't have a given part, students should write "Does not apply" on their papers.
5. Call on different groups to identify the parts found in their books.

EXTENSION:
Try the same activity using fiction books. Include the idea of reading a few paragraphs chosen at random to evaluate the author's style.

Pre-Reading Guide

Pre-reading a book means looking at its parts and deciding if you should read the whole thing. Get a nonfiction book, then use this guide to pre-read it. Answer the questions. Then briefly explain why you would or wouldn't read it.

Titles: All books have a main title. Some have a subtitle that tells about the subject or says who the book is for.
• What are the main and subtitles of the book?
• Just using the title or titles, what do you think the book is mainly about?

Authors/illustrator: If there are two authors, each is called a coauthor. An illustrator creates pictures.
• How many authors wrote your book?
• Does the book give information about who wrote it?

Audience: Most books are written for one type of reader, such as people who already know a little about the topic.
• Who is your book is written for? Why do you think that?

Blurb: If the book has an outer "jacket," that's where you'll find the blurb. It may tell about the contents and the author.
• What's the most important fact you learned from the blurb?

Contents page: This page lists the parts of the book.
• How many chapters does your book have?
• Besides chapters, what else is listed on the contents page?

Copyright: This tells when the book was first published.
• When was the book first copyrighted?

Glossary: This gives definitions of words used in the book.
• On what page does the glossary begin?
• How many words are in the glossary?

Illustrations: These are drawings, maps, and photographs.
• What kinds of illustrations are found in the book?

Index: The index lists topics covered in a book.
• About how many topics does it include?
• What topic has the most pages devoted to it?

 Ten-Minute Real World Reading ©1997 Monday Morning Books, Inc.

SKILL: QUESTIONING

Successful readers have the habit of questioning what they read. You can reinforce this trait by having students brainstorm questions about short passages.

DIRECTIONS:
1. Write a sentence or short paragraph on the board.
For example,

Some experts believe the population of the world will double in the next 100 years.

You'll find more examples on the next page.
2. Ask students, working alone or with a partner, to generate as many questions as they can that relate to the sentence.
For example:
• Who are these experts?
• How do the experts know that the population will double?
• Does it matter if the population doubles?
• Who counts the population of the world?
3. Share the questions orally or by having students post them on the board.

EXTENSION:
Give students short articles from nonfiction books, newspapers, or magazines. Alone or in small groups, have them see how many questions they can brainstorm for each reading.

Question Starters

Niagara Falls is the widest waterfall in the world.

One side of the moon never faces Earth.

English has borrowed more words from French
than from any other language.

In every second, 24 still pictures are flashed on the screen.

Some animals are able to sleep standing up.

When hungry enough, lions will eat their own cubs.

Mice have the same number of bones in their necks
as giraffes.

Bats "see" in the dark by bouncing sounds off objects.

Fish need oxygen as much as land creatures do.

If an octopus loses one of its arms, it will grow back.

Insect blood is not red.

On the moon, you would weigh 1/6 of your weight on Earth.

The sun is closest to Earth in winter and furthest
away in the summer.

The armor worn by a medieval knight weighed about 50
pounds (23 kilograms).

The first bicycles didn't have pedals.

A spider's thread is stronger than a thread of the same size
made of steel.

SKILL: READING RECALL

Reading is more than looking at words. It involves all sorts of thinking skills, including remembering things.

DIRECTIONS:
1. Ahead of time, duplicate and cut apart the Reading Recall Cards, next page.
2. Give each student a copy of the same card.
3. Have students read the material carefully, then turn the cards face down.
4. On their own paper, have students write everything that they can remember on the card. They should double-space (skip every other line) to leave room for filling in material as they remember it.
5. Have students reread the card and list any important ideas and facts that they hadn't recalled.

EXTENSION:
Repeat the activity using other cards. For a variation, show a short, nonfiction video, for example, a nature video, and have students describe it in as much detail as they can.

Reading Recall Cards

Hunting Buried Treasure with Pigs

The truffle is the world's most expensive edible plant. This fungus can sell for more than 100 times the price of apples.

Like other funguses, truffles feed on plant material. They grow underground near the roots of oak trees. The best truffles come from France.

Finding truffles has become an art. Many truffle hunters use trained pigs called "rooting hogs." These pigs can smell the plants three feet (a meter) below the surface. When the pigs begin to grunt and dig into the ground, the farmers quickly push the animals aside. Otherwise, the pigs will devour the crop. That's because pigs love truffles as much as people do.

Do You Carry a Brolly?

"Brolly" is one of its names. So are "bumbershoot" and "parasol." For a while, it was called a "Hanway." That's because in the 1650s, Hanway made this device popular by carrying one around London in rain or shine. Most people call it an umbrella.

Umbrellas have been used since ancient times. A 3000-year-old stone tablet shows a king shaded by one. Similar scenes appear in art from Egypt, Greece, and China.

The fold-up mechanism might seem modern. However, historians found a collapsible umbrella in a Korean tomb more than 2,000 years old! In more recent times, Monet, Renoir, and other famous artists painted all sorts of people carrying umbrellas. How about you?

The New Gas

In 1898, chemists William Ramsay and Morris Travers discovered a colorless, odorless, tasteless gas. They named it "neon," from the Greek word *neos* meaning "new."

The two scientists learned that neon glows red when electricity flows through it. But they had no idea how to use the gas. A few years later, a French physicist, Georges Claude, got the answer. He put the gas into a tube and lit a room with it.

This invention wasn't popular because people didn't like the red color. Then someone suggested using the neon tube for a store sign. The idea was a hit. Soon neon signs were seen throughout the world.

Ten-Minute Real World Reading ©1997 Monday Morning Books, Inc.

READER'S GUIDE

Approaching a Book: There are three ways to read a book:
• *Surface reading*: To get the main idea, focus on the introduction, the ending, plus the contents page, if there is one. Also skim the information printed on the book jacket.
• *Deep reading*: To get as much out of the material as you can, stop from time to time to make notes. Use a dictionary or other references to clarify ideas. Try reading a few passages aloud.
• *Comparative reading*: By reading several books on the same subject, you may gain a deeper understanding than by reading just one book.

Beginnings: Some books start in a puzzling way, but get better as you read more. For this reason, read a few chapters before you decide whether or not to finish a book.

Book Care: In a way, books are like tools. They should be handled thoughtfully.
• *Keep books dry.* Liquid can smear the type and make paper tear easily. It can also encourage mildew, a fungus that discolors the pages. If you must carry a book in the rain, cover it completely. If a book gets wet, dry it with paper towels. Then lay it open in a warm place. After a while, turn to a different part of the book so that all the pages dry. If a library book gets wet, after giving it "first aid," take it to a librarian and point out the problem.
• *Don't break the binding.* The binding is the part of the book that holds the pages together. You can easily damage it by closing a book with a pencil inside or by placing an opened book with the pages facing down.
• *Keep the pages clean.* If you're using a library book or a book owned by someone else, never mark in the book. Write your notes in a separate notebook.
• *Be gentle with the pages.* Don't bend them to keep your place because that will weaken the paper. Instead, use a bookmark.

Dictionary: It's not necessary to look up every word you don't understand. Doing so may cause you to lose track of the main idea. But if you keep a dictionary handy while you read and sometimes look up a word, you'll slowly build a bigger vocabulary.

Eyestrain: When your eyes feel sore, stop reading. If the problem comes back, or if the words seem blurred, have your eyes checked by an eye specialist.

Favorite Author: If you like one book by an author, look for other books by the same person. Usually, you'll be pleased.

Library Organization: In many libraries, fiction books are shelved alphabetically by the author's last name. Nonfiction books are often organized using the Dewey Decimal system. It groups books by topics such as religion, science, art, and history. Each topic has a number range. For example, science books are numbered from 500 to 599. Every book has its own number, like a street address. When you look up a book in the library's catalog, you can find the number, which will lead you to the book.

Lighting: Make sure there is plenty of light falling on the book. The light should come from above or behind you.

Newspapers: Most reporters build their articles around six questions: <u>who?</u>, <u>did what?</u>, <u>how?</u>, <u>where?</u>, <u>when?</u>, and <u>why</u>? To understand an article, look for the answers to these questions.

Note Taking: When reading a book for information, you may want to take notes so that you can remember important facts. This is especially important if you're writing a report. Don't copy large amounts of material. Instead, think about the meaning of the passage, and then translate it into your own words. Try adding an example from your own life.

Ten-Minute Real World Reading ©1997 Monday Morning Books, Inc.

Pacing: Francis Bacon, a famous thinker, once said: "Some books are to be tasted, others to be swallowed, and some few to be chewed and digested." The idea is that you need to adjust your reading speed to fit what you're reading.

• If you need to find a fact in a reference book, it makes sense to skim (read quickly) and not worry about material you don't need.

• If you're trying to understand a scientific experiment or a tricky math problem, slow down. Stop from time to time and think about what you just read. If you don't understand something, reread the passage.

Posture: Sit in a comfortable position. For most people this means sitting in a chair with back support.

Proofreading: When we write something ourselves, we need to check the material carefully, to catch spelling and other mistakes. To do a good job proofreading your own writing or that of someone you know, try the following:

• Read very slowly.

• If something puzzles you, stop and make a note in the margin.

• Watch out for missing words and for extra words.

• If an idea or action is unclear, express it in different words.

• Divide difficult sentences in two. Watch for "run on" sentences that need to be punctuated as two separate sentences.

• Think about paragraphing. In nonfiction, putting different topics into separate paragraphs helps readers understand the ideas. In a story, whenever a different character starts talking, it's best to start a new paragraph.

• Look up the spelling of every word you're not sure of.

• Watch for homonym errors, for example, *too* instead of *to* or *two* and *their* instead of *there* or *they're*.

Purpose: Every piece of writing does one or more of the following jobs: gives facts, gives an opinion, teaches a skill, tells a story, or entertains. Figuring out the purpose can help you better understand what you're reading.

Reading Record: In a journal or notebook, keep track of the books you read. List the title, the author, the date you finished it, and a brief opinion about it. Months or years in the future, you'll find it interesting to discover what you read in the past.

Recommendations: When you find a book that you like, get in the habit of telling people about it. These other readers will often reward you by telling you about a book they liked.

Rereading: Many good books are worth reading more than once. You may be surprised how much you missed the first time.

Psst! You HAVE to read....

Titles: Pay attention to titles. They can give you a big hint about the content or purpose of a piece of writing. For example, *James and the Giant Peach* lets you know who the star of the book is.

Understanding a Book: If you want to check how well you understand what you've read, there's a simple test you can give yourself. It consists of four questions:
• *What is the writing about as a whole?* You should be able to answer this in one or two sentences.
• *What are the most important details, facts, events, or lessons?* You should be able to list several points.
• *Is the material true or believable?* If it's nonfiction, is it up to date? Where did the information come from? If the book is fiction, do the main characters seem to behave in a way that makes sense? You should be able to give examples one way or the other.
• *Is the material important?* First, is it important to you? Did you learn anything from it? Did it open your mind? Is it better than other books on the same subject? Second, would it have value for other people?

ONGOING PROJECTS

The following activities are designed to enrich your overall language arts program. While they can be done as one-time experiences, most work as continuing projects.

Author Mail: Interacting with authors can be a major motivator. The following suggestions may increase the likelihood that students will get a meaningful response:
• Keep the letters short.
• If a reply is desired—say, to answer a question— enclose a self-addressed stamped envelope.
• If everyone in the class wants to write to the same author, send a group-written letter rather than a collection of nearly identical notes.
• Try contacting lesser-known writers. These might include local writers such as newspaper reporters, advertising writers, and poets.

Book Groups: Have four or five students read a book and chat about it chapter by chapter or after they're finished reading the whole thing. An alternative is to have an ongoing book discussion with a pen pal.

Guest Readers: The greater number of readers that students encounter, the more important reading will seem to them. Invite the principal, fellow teachers, high school students, and others to read for your class. As an example, the editor of the high school newspaper might read a few editorials and then discuss the steps in putting out a newspaper.

Home Reading Hour: To create a community of readers, invite all parents to set aside a few minutes nightly, during which time everyone in the family can read silently or for the other family members.

Library Odyssey: After students learn about the Dewey Decimal System (used to organize books in many libraries), challenge students to read a book in each of the ten categories, and also to read from the major fiction genres.

News Show: Produce a weekly or monthly current events round-up. This can take the form of a tape-recorded radio show, or for a bigger challenge, as a video-taped TV program.

Poetry/Prose Reading: Invite students to perform their poems or stories in class, for other classes, and on tape for parents. Or hold a reading in a public place, such as the library or a bookstore.

Proofreading Service: Arrange for students to proofread the work of younger children. This help can be oral, or given as margin notes that identify good points and problems. An editor can make suggestions but should not change the writer's draft. That's the author's responsibility.

Read Around the World and Across Time: Books can act as magic carpets and as time machines that take readers to exotic settings. Devise a program in which students visit a dozen places via books.

Renaissance Readers: Have students identify topics they know nothing about, and then read books in that field. The goal is to demonstrate that reading is a powerful tool for overcoming gaps in one's information background.

Review Column: Have students take turns reviewing books for the school newspaper or, if you're online, the school home page.

Time Capsule: Ask each student to contribute one or more titles to a "favorite books" list that will be left as a gift for next year's students. To add pizzazz, each student might tape a short passage from a book.

    Ten-Minute Real World Reading ©1997 Monday Morning Books, Inc.

CREATIVE BOOK REPORTS

Newspaper-style Reviews:
To create authentic reviews, students must go beyond plot or content summaries. Checklists can help:
• Overall opinion: "Although it had some exciting scenes, overall I found the book boring and even silly."
• Goal of the book: "This science fiction novel creates a surprising picture of life in the twenty-fifth century."
• Excerpts that reveal a book's strengths or weaknesses: an example of memorable dialogue, a picturesque description, or—on the negative side—a fact error.

Key Word Essays:
The student brainstorms words that the book evokes. For example, with *Where the Wild Things Are*, the list might include: *strange*, *scary*, and *exciting*. The reader chooses one word as the focus for an essay about the book.

Character Perspectives:
Students write from a character's point of view, for example: "My name is Dorothy. Let me tell you about my experiences in Oz." A related option is for the reviewer to do a mock interview with a character:
 Q: Alice, what was your worst moment in Wonderland?
 A: The time when I started shrinking was scary.

Advertisements:
Students prepare 60-second radio commercials selling their books. They can then read them to the class, or swap papers and read each other's commercials aloud.

Sequels:
One way to demonstrate familiarity with a text is to write a sequel to it. An example would be *Return to Oz* or *The Giant Peach Comes Back*. A related form is the parody, for example, *Nightmare in Wonderland.*

Models and Dioramas:
Readers construct 3-D displays that represent important objects, ideas, scenes, or actions from the reading. Labels explain the significance of the presentations.